Little Mitchie

IT TASTES SOUR

Kim Thompson

CREATING YOUNG NONFICTION READERS

Little Mitchie books spark curiosity and support early nonfiction reading for students in Grades 2-3. Designed to build vocabulary, support second language learners, and prepare readers for middle-grade content, each book includes helpful tips for parents and educators to build confidence and deepen understanding of the world.

TIPS FOR READING NONFICTION WITH BEGINNING READERS

Talk about Nonfiction

Begin by explaining that nonfiction books give us information that is true. The book will be organized around a specific topic or idea, and we may learn new facts through reading.

Look at the Parts

Most nonfiction books have helpful features. Our *Little Mitchie* titles include color photographs and graphic aids, a table of contents, a glossary, and an index. Share the purpose of these features with your reader.

Color Photos and Graphic Aids

A lot of information can be found by "reading" photos, charts, maps, and other graphic aids found within nonfiction texts. Help your reader learn more about the different ways information can be displayed.

Table of Contents

Located at the front of the book, this list shows the big ideas within the text and the page numbers where they can be found.

Glossary

Located at the back of the book, the glossary defines key words and phrases that are related to the topic. These words and phrases can be found in the text in colored type.

Index

Located at the back of the book, an index is an alphabetical list of topics and the page numbers where they can be found.

With a little help and guidance about reading nonfiction, you can feel good about introducing a young reader to the world of *Little Mitchie* nonfiction books.

Little Mitchie is an imprint of:

Mitchell Lane
PUBLISHERS

2001 SW 31st Avenue
Hallandale, FL 33009
mitchelllanepub.com

First Edition, 2027.

Author: Kim Thompson
Designer: Bobbie Houser

Library of Congress Cataloging-in-Publication Data
Title: It Tastes Sour / by Kim Thompson

Description: Hallandale, FL :
Mitchell Lane Publishers, [2027]

Identifiers:
ISBN 979-8-89260-857-2 (library bound)
ISBN 979-8-89260-954-8 (eBook)

Library of Congress Control Number: 2026935746

PHOTO CREDITS
Shutterstock: Photoongraphy, cover, 1, 3, 4, 10, 18; Irina Mikhailichenko, 5; New Africa, 6, 11, 12; Christina Desitriviantie, 7; casanisa, 8; Monkey Business Images, 15; AYO Production, 16; BearFotos, 19; Nungning20, 20; FotoHelin, 22.

TABLE OF CONTENTS

Chapter One

A SOUR TASTE . . . 4

Chapter Two

THE SCIENCE OF SOURNESS . . . 10

Chapter Three

EATING SOUR FOODS . . . 18

RECIPE: SOUR GRAPES . . . 22

GLOSSARY . . . 23

FURTHER READING . . . 24

ON THE INTERNET . . . 24

INDEX . . . 24

Chapter One

A SOUR TASTE

Sip fresh grapefruit juice. Bite into a crunchy pickle. Eat a spoonful of plain yogurt. As you get a taste, your face might scrunch up. Your lips may pucker.

These foods have different shapes, colors, and textures. They have one flavor in common, though. They are all sour!

Some sour foods are found in nature. Many fruits are sour. There are **citrus** fruits like lemons, limes, and kumquats. There are tart green apples, cranberries, and cherries.

TASTY TiDBiT
Bilimbi may be the sourest food. People who eat this tropical fruit say the flavor makes their jaws tense up in pain!

Some foods are sour because of the way they are prepared. People **ferment** foods by adding **bacteria** or **yeast**. The tiny creatures break down sugars. They produce **acids** that make the food taste sour.

Yogurt is fermented milk. Some **vinegar** is fermented apple juice. Sauerkraut and kimchi are fermented vegetables.

Chapter Two

THE SCIENCE OF SOURNESS

Sour tastes are sharp, tangy, and bright. The punch of flavor happens because sour foods are acidic. They have a low pH. That means they contain many **hydrogen ions**.

TASTY TIDBIT

pH is measured on a scale from 0 (most acidic) to 14 (most basic). Lemons have a pH of about 2. Lemon juice is so acidic that it can power a battery!

TASTY TIDBIT
Many people love sour candies. Some are coated with artificial citric acid and malic acid. This gives them strong pucker power!

Look closely at your tongue. It is covered with bumps. These are **papillae**. They are filled with tiny structures called taste buds.

Taste buds are shaped like pockets. They have tiny hairs sticking out. These microvilli sense acids. They send **signals** to your brain. Your brain knows that the taste is sour.

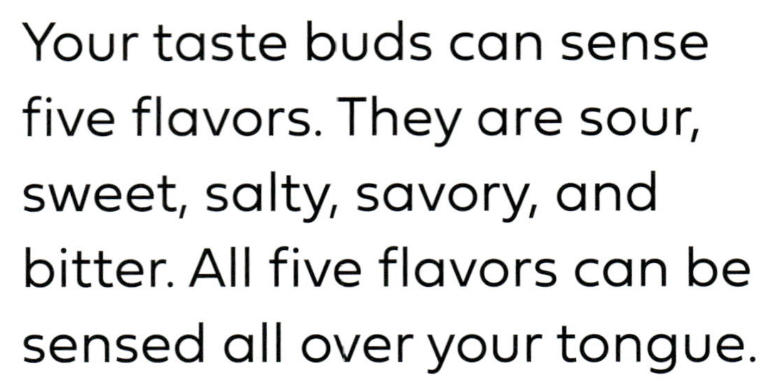

Your taste buds can sense five flavors. They are sour, sweet, salty, savory, and bitter. All five flavors can be sensed all over your tongue.

TASTY TIDBIT

Babies have about 30,000 taste buds. Adults have less than 10,000. That's why flavors taste stronger to kids than they do to adults.

Have you ever noticed that having a stuffy nose makes it harder to taste your food? That's because your nose helps you taste. Food smells reach sense **receptors** in your nose. They send flavor information to your brain.

Chapter Three

EATING SOUR FOODS

Humans need vitamin C. Lemons and other sour foods contain this important vitamin. That could be why we like to eat them.

Another reason to like acidic foods is that they are usually safe to eat. Harmful bacteria cannot grow on them. Fermenting food is a way to preserve it.

Many sour foods are healthy. They have vitamins and fiber. They have good bacteria and other things your body needs. Go ahead and enjoy sour treats. Just be prepared to pucker!

SOUR GRAPES

Ingredients:

Three small boxes of gelatin mix with sour flavors such as lemon, lime, orange, watermelon, or blue raspberry

Two lemons

One bunch green grapes

Toothpicks

Directions:

1. Pour each gelatin mix into a shallow bowl.
2. Ask an adult to help you cut the lemons in half. Squeeze their juice into a small bowl.
3. Pick the grapes off their stems.
4. Poke a toothpick into a grape. Hold the toothpick as you dip the grape into the lemon juice and then roll it in one of the gelatin flavors until completely covered. Put it on a plate or tray. Repeat with as many grapes as you like.
5. Refrigerate the grapes for several hours or freeze them overnight. Pop them in your mouth to pucker up and enjoy the sour taste!

GLOSSARY

acids (AS-ids) chemicals that contain hydrogen ions, usually dissolve in water, have a sour taste, and have a pH less than seven

bacteria (bak-TEER-ee-uh) microscopic, single-celled living things

citrus (SIT-ruhs) a type of fruit, such as an orange or a grapefruit, that is acidic, sour, and juicy

ferment (fur-MENT) to use bacteria or yeast to break down the sugars in a substance to form acids or alcohols

hydrogen ions (HYE-druh-juhn EYE-ahnz) particles of the chemical hydrogen that have a positive charge

papillae (puh-PILL-ee) small bumps on the tongue that contain taste buds

receptors (ri-SEP-turz) nerve endings that are sensitive to stimuli in the environment such as smells

signals (SIG-nuhlz) chemical and electrical messages that get sent to the brain through the body's nervous system

vinegar (VIN-i-gur) a sour liquid, usually made from fermented fruit juice, that is used to flavor, pickle, and preserve foods

yeast (yeest) a single-celled fungus that is used to ferment foods and make bread rise

FURTHER READING

DePalma, Kate. *The Bread Pet.* Barefoot Books, 2020.

Highlights. *The Ultimate Science Cookbook for Kids: A Cookbook for Young Scientists That Transforms the Kitchen into a Food Lab for Learning.* Highlights Press, 2025.

ON THE INTERNET

Mystery Science: What Makes Some Candy So Sour?
youtube.com/watch?v=FKVxeqgOZww
Learn why sour candy makes your mouth pucker.

Science Buddies: A Simple Sourness Detector
scientificamerican.com/article/a-simple-sourness-detector
This science experiment uses baking soda to detect foods in your kitchen that are sour.

INDEX

acids 8, 10–13, 19
bacteria 8, 19, 21
brain 13, 17
fermentation 8, 9, 19
lemons 6, 11, 18, 22
nose 17
pH 10, 11
taste buds 13, 14
tongue 13, 14
vitamin C 18